PRINCE WILLIAM
PRINCE WILLIAM
PRINCE WILLIAM
PRINCE WILLIAM
PRINCE WILLIAM
PRINCE WILLIAM
PRINCE WILLIAM
PRINCE WILLIAM
PRINCE WILLIAM
PRINCE WILLIAM
PRINCE WILLIAM
PRINCE WILLIAM
PRINCE WILLIAM
PRINCE WILLIAM
PRINCE WILLIAM

Published by:

Central Park Publishing, LLC

30 Rockefeller Plaza, Suite 2829, New York, New York, 10112

Text copyright© 1998 by Brook Walters

Book design by E. DeSear

ISBN#: 0-9664074-0-7

Printed in the United States of America

May 1998

# PRINCE WILLIAM
## A JOURNEY TO THE THRONE

Forget that he is Heir Apparent to the British throne, has

a personal valet or even has tea with the Queen of

England (his granny) every Sunday.

# HIS ROYAL HIGHNESS PRINCE WILLIAM

His Royal Highness, Prince William is one down-to-

earth dude — one more reason to love him! "I'm normal

...I bleed when cut, just like you," he says.

Prince William Attends The Spice Girls' London Premier of
their new movie "SPICE WORLD".

15-year-old Wills (one of his many adorable nicknames, like "His Naughtiness") has been called "The most handsome royal." Who would argue? At 6'2" with sandy blonde hair and dreamy hazel eyes, he's every girl's dream boy — the perfect pinup. But, believe it or not (Not!), he's painfully shy about his luscious looks and actually pokes fun at his movie star status.

# THE PERFECT PINUP

"William takes it all in good heart. He's more than capable of taking the rise out of himself," says a confidante about his quick and self-effacing humor. His school chums call him "Dreamboat Willy;" without his humble ways, it might be hard for the most famous teenager in the world to shrug that one off!

Prince William at Balmoral, Scotland.

# DREAMBOAT WILLY

Born on June 21, 1982 at 9:03 p.m. at St. Mary's Hospital in

Paddington, London — 8 hours after a solar eclipse — His Royal

Highness, Prince William Arthur Philip Louis Windsor of Wales

(whew!) is considered to be both a Gemini and a Cancer since

he has a borderline birthday (some astrologists cut off Gemini

at the 20th of June, others at the 21st).

Prince William skiing at Whistler, British Columbia.

The baby babe was Christened on August 4, 1982 at

Buckingham Palace, the royal home of his grandparents,

Queen Elizabeth II and Prince Philip.

# LIFE AT ETON

So far, he has attended four schools: Mrs. Mynor's Nursery

school in West London, Wetherby School in Kensington,

London, Ludgrove School in Wokingham and is now in his

third year at Eton College (Boarding School to Brits); an

exclusive, all-boys school with more than 1,200 students.

The cost?  A whopping $25,000 a year!

Prince William on the crew team at Eton.

# OXFORD-BOUND

Eton is equipped with two swimming pools, dozens of soccer, rugby

and cricket fields — even a golf course.  But, don't be fooled, he's got

a strict daily regimen: breakfast at 8 a.m., chapel service, then morning

classes.  After lunch, at about 1:30 p.m., he takes a much loved sports

break before classes resume at 4 p.m.


Wills lives in Manor House, an ivy-covered dorm with 49 other guys

and is getting psyched up to go off to college.  First, though, he

needs to pass a series of nasty national exams — the GCSEs —

required by all British students who plan to attend University.  Some

even say he's Oxford-bound...

Prince William with fellow classmates at Eton College.

The beautiful Brit is an awesome athlete who plays virtually

all sports: skiing, tennis, soccer, hockey, rafting, swimming,

mountain biking, go-cart racing and rowing on the Thames.

# AWESOME ATHLETE

But there's no sport he digs more than shooting. "He takes

part in Beagling (hunting hares with beagles) at school.

Apparently quite keen," said a former Eton student.

Prince William Jet Skiing in St. Tropez, France.

# MAYBE HE'LL BE THE NEXT PICASSO

Even though he's left-handed, Wills is definitely right-brained — creative — and is an excellent painter. Who knows? Maybe he'll be the next Picasso! Until then, he's just trying to be a regular guy who hangs out with his buddies, watches MTV and grooves to good tunes like techno, the bands Pulp and Oasis, the theme song to Mission Impossible and his favorite, The Spice Girls (he's particularly flipped for "Baby Spice").

Prince William at Eton College.

# HE ENJOYS THE NIGHT LIFE

He enjoys the night life, goes to London disco parties, even boozes

it up now and then (he's been known to nurse an occasional hang-

over after a night in his schoolmates rooms). He logs in some driving

time (though he won't get his driver's license until he's 17) when

Prince Charles lets him take his Land Rover for a spin at Balmoral,

the family estate in Scotland. The royal rebel even broke the rules

when at age 13 he announced he would not join the Royal Navy like

his family members before him.

Prince William on winter ski holiday with
family at Klosters, Switzerland.

He prefers boxers over briefs and loves to chow down on hamburgers, pasta, chocolate, venison and fruit salad. What does he wash it all down with? Coke or red wine.

# PREFERS BOXERS OVER BRIEFS

Though Wills has not dated — yet — he reportedly has his royal eye on a lucky gal named Zara Simmonds. Discussions are already underway as to how he can maintain his much-needed privacy when the dating day comes.

Prince William visits Pacific Space Center in Vancover, British Columbia, March 1998.

Photo: Camera Press

# COULD HE MARRY AN AMERICAN?

Could he marry an American?  YES!  But, she must meet two requirements:  She must be Protestant and not divorced.

In private, Wills is outgoing, caring and hangs out with his own tight-knit group of friends.  In public, Wills is shy, skittish and has a disdain for the media — never more so than after Princess Diana's — his beloved mum — tragic death in late August of 1997.

Prince William at Balmoral, Scotland.

25

Wills and Di were tight, she exposed him to the fun side of royal life.

They vacationed in the Caribbean, ate at trendy restaurants, dirt-biked

at Goldie Hawn's Colorado ranch and — get this — when he told her

that he fancied Cindy Crawford, she invited the supermodel to tea!

# CINDY CRAWFORD

He relied almost exclusively on his mother for support and advice in

his sometimes rocky fifteen years. She was his anchor. Diana even

turned to Wills for guidance when he advised her to auction off her

gorgeous gowns at Christie's Auction House. Since Diana's death,

Wills has tried to cope, but it's been a rough road.

Prince William SCUBA diving on summer holiday.

# TIGGY LEGGE-BOURKE IS A SOURCE OF COMFORT FOR THE YOUNG PRINCE.

Loved and supported by Diana's siblings — Lady Sarah McCorquodale, Lady Jane Fellowes and Earl Charles Spencer — Wills and his 13-year-old brother Prince Harry chat with their aunts and uncle on the tele almost daily.

His surrogate mother since Wills' parents divorce, Tiggy Legge-Bourke, Prince Charles' former Social Secretary, is still, and always will be, a source of comfort for the young prince.

Prince William with Prince Henry visit Pacific Space Center in Vancover, British Columbia.

# PRINCE WILLIAM HAS DEALT WITH MORE HEARTACHE THAN MANY TEENS

At his all-too-sensitive age, Prince William has dealt with more heartache than many teens. His parent's very public, bitter divorce was overwhelming for the young royal (as a reminder of his parent's happier days, he kept Di's diamond-and-sapphire engagement ring). But, with the poise he inherited from his mother, The Prince of Hearts moved forward and re-adjusted to his new, split life.

Prince William greeting well wishers at Kensington Palace after he arrived to view tributes left in memory of his mother

# WILLS HAS A SHARP AWARENESS OF HIS ROYAL DESTINY

Wills has his mother's shy self-confidence and his father's sharp awareness of his royal destiny. Despite his intense emotions, he fulfills his royal family duties, like his first official outing after Diana's death; his grandparent's 50th wedding anniversary celebration at Westminster Abbey, where his mother's funeral service took place.

Prince William at Balmoral, Scotland.

Prince Charles is a cool dad.  Wills spends 38 weeks a year at Eton and since Diana's death, the rest of the time with him.  All three royal guys— Wills, Harry, Prince Charles — and Will's black Labrador, Widgeon, are planning to move to York House, a five-bedroom pad on the grounds of London's St. James's Palace, complete with a computer and a pool table.

# GRACE & CHARM

When the time comes to be throned — maybe not before he turns 40 — Prince William will be hailed as King William V of England.  Some say he is "the last best hope of the British Monarchy."  With so much pressure that rides on his shoulders, he will, no doubt, handle it as he always does — with grace, charm...and a winning smile.

Prince William at Balmoral, Scotland.

Photo © Rex USA Ltd.

# INTERESTING FACTS ABOUT
# PRINCE WILLIAM

| | |
|---|---|
| BORN | June 21, 1982, 7 lbs. 10 oz. St. Mary's Hospital in London |
| STAR SIGN | Cancer (borderline Gemini) |
| ADDRESSES | Eton College, St. James Palace, and Highgrove |
| HEIGHT/WEIGHT | 6'2", about 130 lbs. |
| EYES/HAIR | Hazel, sandy blond |
| TITLE | His Royal Highness Prince William of Wales |
| FULL NAME | Prince William Arthur Philip Louis Mountbatten-Windsor |
| PETS | Black lab, Widgeon (4 years) |
| LOVES | Fast cars, sports (shooting, tennis, hockey, skiing), painting, Coke, red wine, pasta, hamburgers, chocolate, venison, fruit salad, Thames River swimming, rafting, discos, techno music, Spice Girls. |
| INTERESTING FACTS: | Prince Charles and Prince William are forbidden to fly on the same plane together. If the plane were to go down, both heirs to the throne would be lost. |
| | Prince William is left-handed |
| | As king, he will be called William V |

Prince William on ski vacation at
Whistler Mountain, British Columbia.